Early Diesels on the LMS and LMR

Compiled by Kevin Robertson

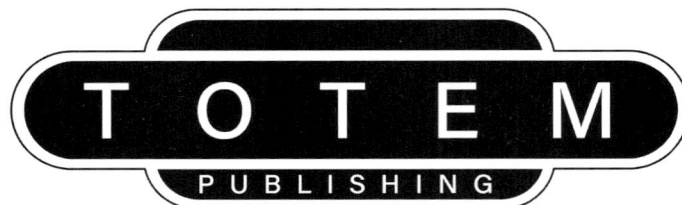

TOTEM
PUBLISHING

© Images and design: The Transport Treasury 2022. Text Kevin Robertson

ISBN-978-1-913893-12-5

First Published in 2022 by Transport Treasury Publishing Ltd. 16 Highworth Close, High Wycombe, HP13 7PJ

Totem Publishing, an imprint of Transport Treasury Publishing.

www.ttpublishing.co.uk

Printed in Tarxien, Malta by Gutenberg Press Ltd.

'*Early Diesels on The LMS and LMR*' is one of a series of books on specialist transport subjects published in strictly limited numbers and produced under the Totem Publishing imprint using material principally only available at The Transport Treasury.

Front cover: LMS No 10000, the only main line diesel locomotive in Britain to operate under the auspices of a pre-nationalisation railway. Completed at Derby just two weeks before nationalisation, in consequence it receiving tread plates at the door to the cab bearing the initials LMS as well as similar letters on the bodyside. It is seen here probably not long after building and with perhaps a loco inspector or 'technical bod' on the footsteps. Notice the rainstrip above the cab window and door.

Frontispiece (1): No 10000 alongside what could even have turned out to be its nemesis, 'Duchess' pacific No 6256 Sir William A. Stanier F.R.S. As it was the steam engine would end up being usurped by the 'new kid on the block'. Nos 6256 and sister engine 6257 were the final pair of pacifics built for the LMS and incorporated a number of detail differences, roller bearings for example, intended to bring them as up to date as possible whilst keeping to the basic Stephenson steam engine design. Not for the LMS Chief Mechanical Engineer, H. G. Ivatt, was there the kind of experimentation going on simultaneously as was taking place on the Southern at Brighton at this time. Had the LMS survived, we might well have seen formal trials between No 6256, pitted against the pairing of 10000/10001. As it was BR decided instead to hold exchange trials between steam engines drawn from the pre-nationalisation companies. We will never know how in an effective comparison test these two differing forms of traction might have fared against each other. Euston, 18 December 1947.

Rear cover: On 11 June 1949, the pair are seen leaving Euston with the second man of No 10000 looking back to see all is well. The driver's position was on the left of the cab.

Introduction

Britain's first main line diesel locomotive arrived on the scene courtesy of the LMS in December 1947. Numbered 10000 and displayed in striking black livery with a narrow aluminium band running around the complete bodywork, it set the scene for what was to be a revolution in railway motive power. At the time never intended to replace steam, No 10000 and its twin sister 10001, which appeared shortly after in 1948, were seen very much as prototypes and when run together in multiple could match and in some respects exceed the output of an LMS 'Duchess' pacific.

It has to be said the LMS had been in the forefront of diesel traction on the railways dating back as far as 1931/2 when the unusual step was taken of converting a steam engine to a diesel! This involved a former Midland Railway 0-6-0 which was stripped to the frames with the boiler and firebox replaced by a 400hp Paxman diesel engine having hydrostatic transmission (a fluid transmission whereby fluid is delivered from a pump attached to the diesel engine to a separate engine which in turn drives the wheels). The original steam era wheels were retained with a crankshaft type arrangement emerging between one pair of driving wheels, to which was attached a connection to the coupling rods. The whole was surmounted by what has been well described by Colin Marsden and others as a 'shoe box' type body; perhaps the originals of the later oft used phrase for

(2): The Fell diesel outside Derby works. Originally designated with the 4-8-4 wheel arrangement, the innermost pairs of wheels were soon separated after which the engine became a 4-4-4-4, as is seen here. This took place sometime after six months of running in 1952 and was related to bearing issues in the coupling rods allied to stress between the gearbox and the coupling rods. Previous difficulties in traffic from this issue were then eliminated.

The Fell could certainly not be said to particularly attractive, the necessary but unsightly radiator grill at either end not helping. It certainly never had the benefit of external design input from the later Design Panel. Had the design been perpetuated there was talk of roof mounted or side radiators instead.

In at least one contemporary technical journal has the number of the engine referred to as being 10,100, likely a misinterpretation from the correct 10100.

'modern' motive power as being little more than a 'box on wheels'.

Trials with No 1831 were not entirely satisfactory; the LNER's first venture into diesel in 1933 with a prototype to an Armstrong Whitworth design was similarly short lived, as after little more than a year the crankcase exploded and it never worked again.

Diesel might have had a shaky start but it would quickly bounce back as more manufacturers came upon the scene. Hunslet for example producing a 150hp 21 ton machine; it was only a matter of time before the advantages of the diesel came to be realised and in consequence no less than seven prototypes were delivered to the LMS for evaluation in just a two year period, 1933/4. These emanated from four different builders and included six different power units. Standardisation was clearly not on the agenda at the time, but then neither was it on the minds of BR a quarter of a century later. These different types are illustrated on the pages that follow.

The number of different diesel shunting types running around on the LMS thus exceeded those on any of the other companies. Elsewhere it was only on the GWR that the potential advantages of diesel traction had been taken seriously at the same time, with the introduction of a series of single vehicle railcars intended for express and also cross-country routes. In the case of the latter their popularity quickly exceeded their capability and it was not long before some services which had been given over from steam to diesel were forced to revert to steam again for no other reason than simple passenger numbers.

To return to the LMS, the success of diesel shunters in general, crewed by one man, able to work for long periods without the need for servicing and refuelling, and available at the turn of a key, naturally led to consideration of the diesel engine for use in a main line engine. Perhaps if WW2 had not intervened we might have seen a diesel prototype sooner, but development was in stages and it was really not until a power unit coupled to an electric generator and so able to output a realistic horse power that matters really started to accelerate – almost literally.

What follows is a brief pictorial portrayal of that journey, from steam conversion, to shunter prototypes and then the final big leap to main line engines.

In this latter category we are including a glimpse at that fascinating 4-8-4 (later 4-4-4-4), the 'Fell' diesel mechanical. This was part of the final building programme authorised by the LMS on 29 October 1947 and so qualifies as an LMS design.

At this stage, 1947, work on the two main line diesel-electric engines, Nos 10000 and 10001 was already well advanced and so it may well have been this was an attempt to see which type of transmission would afford the best advantage in service.

The LMS diesel story is a fascinating glimpse into the perceived future by a forward looking railway company brave enough to recognise that the steam engine whilst having many advantages also had its disadvantages. We can only speculate where and how that journey might have led had Nationalisation not taken place.

Kevin Robertson   Berkshire 2021

Bibliography:

Diesel Pioneers. David N Clough. Published Ian Allan 2005.
LMS Diesel locomotives and Railcars. E V Richards. Published by the RCTS 1996.
Prototype Locomotives. Robert Tufnell. Published David & Charles 1985.
The British Internal Combustion Locomotive 1894-1940. Brian Webb. David & Charles 1973.
The Diesel Shunter. Colin Marsden OPC. 2003
The Fell Diesel Mechanical Locomotive. Published Fell Developments, undated.
Top-Link locomotives. Norman McKillop. Published Thomas Nelson and Sons 1957
In addition the author acknowledgements the assistance of Gerry Nichols, the Stephenson Locomotive Society, and also John Wenyon.

(3): From a slightly different angle to that seen on the frontispiece but clearly on the same occasion, and obviously at Euston, the diesel has appropriately enough pulled ahead of the steam engine. Livery was LNWR black except for the bogies which were silver/ aluminium. This latter colouring was hardly appropriate to the rigours of normal traffic - but it did look good when freshly applied. The numerals were raised and chromed as were the cab handrails. Similar handrails fitted to the first (G)WR gas turbine in 1949/50 were found to be too slippery when wet and were replaced. Did the same thing happen on Nos 10000/10001? Inset (4): Driver Len Pile of Camden depot at Euston prior to working the down 1.35pm to Carlisle. The days of single-manning were still well in the future and a fireman (second man) was still required to tend to the train steam heat boiler.

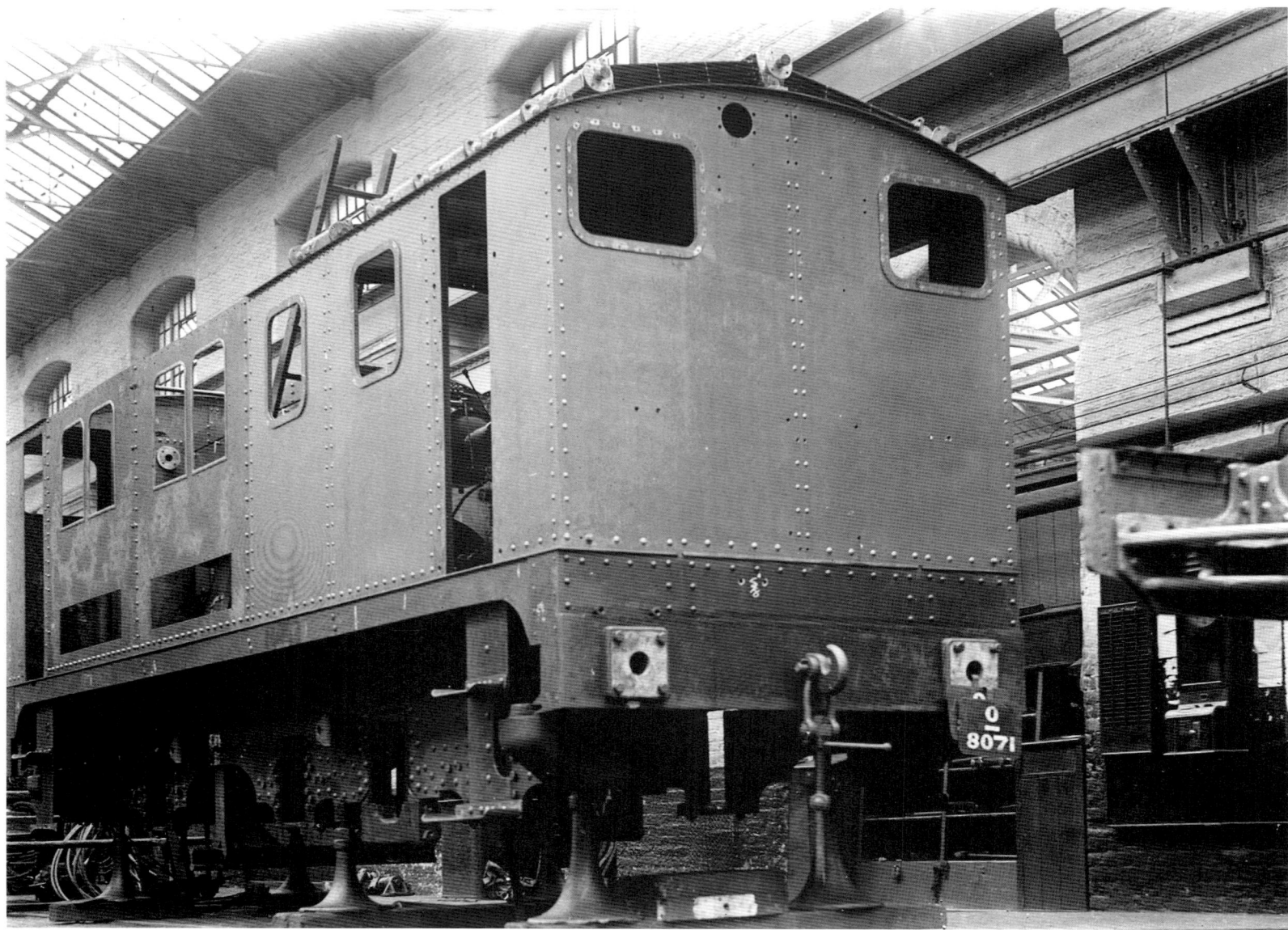

Opposite (5): The first LMS diesel shunting engine. This is the former Midland Railway 0-6-0 steam engine No 1361 in the course of conversion to a diesel. Take note it was not a mixed 'steam-diesel' machine as just the frames and wheels from the steam engine were reused. Inside it is just possible to view part of the replacement diesel engine. Taken at Derby sometime between October 1931 and November 1932, it was deemed to remain a one-off. The idea of potentially utilising parts from a steam engine in a more modern form of traction would surface again in the early 1960s when, rumour had it, the GT3 gas-turbine, had it gone into volume production, would have seen the frames from BR and possibly Stanier Class 5 engines reused.

Above (6): After an operational life of just over three years, No 1831, as it was renumbered in diesel guise, was withdrawn in 1936 and stored before being taken into departmental stock in 1939 and converted into a (non self-propelled) mobile power unit. With there no longer being any need for a driver, alterations were also made to the bodywork as seen. Now as MPU3 it lasted until August 1951.

Top (7): Following trials with an 0-4-0 diesel shunter from late 1934 onwards, the LMS ordered four 0-6-0 diesel shunting engines from the Hunslet Engine Company. Externally all four were similar although there was certainly detail variation with the cabs - as seen here between this and the view below, but what was particularly interesting was that all four differed internally. No 7051 (later renumbered 7401) came with a six-cylinder MAN 150hp engine operating at 900rpm. It also had a four-speed gearbox allowing for a top speed of 30mph but at such speed tractive effort would understandably be limited. It was active first at Leeds (probably Leeds was selected as this was also the town where the builders were based) but like other diesel locomotives moved to Government (War Department) use in 1939. Returned to the LMS between mid-1941 and August 1944, it was again requisitioned for WD use from the latter date until August 1944. No 7051 now entered its final spell with the LMS which lasted until December 1945 when it was withdrawn and returned to the Hunslet Engine Company.

Bottom (8): Numerically the next in the series, No 7402 was fitted with an 8-cylinder McLaren-Benz engine producing 150hp at 1,1000rpm. Unlike later diesels which were started by means of compressed air, the engine on No 7402 required a separate two-cylinder petrol engine worked from the cab which in turn rotated the crankshaft of the diesel until it fired. At this point the petrol engine was disconnected and turned off. A Hunslet gearbox and multiple disc clutch were fitted, connected by a Hardy-Spicer coupling. It was restricted to shunting having a top speed of just 8 mph. No 7402 worked at Leeds until August 1940 when it moved to War Department control. Following a spell with the Air Ministry at Stafford it returned to the LMS at Leeds in February 1942 but then moved again, still under LMS control, to Nottingham. Colin Marsden, in his excellent work The Diesel Shunter (OPC 2003), then speaks of the locomotive being sold by Hunslet to the Admiralty in December 1943 which implies either the LMS had at some stage transferred ownership back to the makers or it had been on long term loan/ hire from them. Whatever, after the end of 1943 the remaining life of the former No 7402 (renumbered as well by the military) is outside the scope of our text although suffice to say it spent the last three years of its life shunting at the Birds scrapyard at Long Marsden, where it would eventually suffer a terminal mechanical failure and was itself scrapped there in 1969. Incidentally, No 7403 of the quartet (not illustrated) had a 6-cylinder 150hp sleeve-valve diesel engine.

(9): In the same year, 1934, came No 7057, built in Belfast by Messrs Harland & Wolfe, a firm certainly better known for its maritime construction including of course the ill-fated White Star vessel the *Titantic*. Marsden comments that this is the only Irish built locomotive to see service in Britain although of course there have been several (unrelated to the present text) locomotives that moved the other way. No 7057 arrived on the LMS in 1935 but it was not to be until the end of 1936 that the engine entered service; this following problems during the testing phase. The engine was fitted with a two-stroke diesel known as a 'Harlandic' and which was also the name given by the builders to their railway division. The engine transmission was connected to a two-speed gearbox by means of a hydraulic coupling with the gearbox driving the front axle via a worm drive. Allocated initially to Chester, it was later at Heysham but was sold back to the manufacturer in January 1945 having been out of service for the previous 12 months. It is possible the illustration seen here was taken during that time. Again its subsequent history is out of scope but suffice to say it was regauged for service in Ireland and remained in use until April 1965.

284651

Opposite (10): Up to now, LMS policy and experience with diesel shunters had been limited to locomotives having mechanical transmission and of limited engine size. This would now change with the introduction into service in 1933 of an 0-6-0 from the manufacturer Armstrong Whitworth and which was rated at 250hp. It is seen here at an unreported location. Little information appears to exist on this machine although it was known to have had a large fuel capacity and consequently could be used as a shunter for up to a week at a time without the need to refuel.

Top (11): Before moving on to the development of the diesel-electric shunter, including those with jackshaft drive, we should mention this unusual and unique machine. It must also be remembered that in what was a totally new arena, different manufacturers were pitting their own products against the opposition in an attempt to gain favour, hence odd prototypes were made and loaned to various railway companies. This particular machine was identified with the name *Vulcan* (the same name as would be carried on an 'Austerity' 2-8-0 years later). As might be expected, it came from the Vulcan Foundry and was fitted with a 275hp Vulcan-Frichs diesel engine. It was with the LMS from 1936 until passing into War Department use and eventually seeing service in the former Yugoslavia. It is seen here in somewhat grimy condition, UK/Europe (?), and with the interesting feature of having glass panels to the tops of the engine access doors. The protrusion immediately ahead of the cab was a central chimney. As with so many of the contemporary diesel shunters, in outline there was often a distinct similarity in some areas to steam, in this case reference the cab.

Bottom (12):Progression to a diesel engine with electric transmission occurred in 1935/36 with ten locomotives ordered to a new design. Fitted with an Armstrong Sulzer power unit and a single traction motor, the final drive was via a jackshaft and side rods; the jackshaft principal being the preferred propulsion as indeed it would be for some years to come. Seen here is No 7063 with a steam relic of past days just creeping into view on the extreme right. As with most diesel shunters of the time, a standard 3-link coupling was fitted. Armstrong Whitworth chose to leave locomotive building in 1937 and the way was thus clear for English Electric to fill the void.

12024

12005
5353

Opposite top (13):Seen from a sideways angle the extra length created by the jackshaft is apparent. This is the former LMS No 7111, now British Railways No 12024, dating from 1939. Livery in BR days was overall BR black but a few in the series did manage to survive long enough to be painted in BR green with accompanying yellow / black ends.

Opposite bottom (14): Sister machine 12005, formerly LMS No 7082, at an unknown depot. The length of the actual jack shaft is interesting and one may perhaps wonder why this was not instead connected to the centre driving wheels to produce a more even torque across front and rear axles. No doubt there was a valid engineering reason! Notice too the works plate on the cab and sand boxes. At this stage, and for some years to come, there were no separate servicing facilities and the diesels had to take their turn with steam being maintained either in the none too clean environs of the steam shed or exposed to the elements outside.

Above (15): This time it is No 12025, the former LMS 7112. This engine, built by the LMS at Derby, entered service in February 1942 and spent time at Carlisle, Crewe and Speke Junction. Considered non-standard by BR, the end came in November 1967 and it was subsequently broken up by the Slag Reduction Co at their Rotherham site.

(16): In 1936 we have what was destined to be the basis for the standard design of diesel-electric shunter in years to come, the 350hp shunter, although it must be said the engines were originally rated at just 300hp. The jack shaft has also now gone. Ten were built but again as might be expected, most – nine in fact – were requisitioned for the war effort. For reasons that are not totally clear, just three passed into BR ownership, No 7069, likely seen here when new, not being one of them. The large steps at the front were a feature of many early shunters, intended to give shunting and yard staff a (relatively) safe place to stand and hold on whilst the locomotive was moving.

(17): One of three Hawthorn Leslie machines of 1936, fitted with an English Electric power plant that passed into BR ownership. No 7076 became BR 12001. It was allocated to Crewe and lasted until 1962 being eventually broken up by BR at Horwich. As with all the shunters, to facilitate shunting on a curved track, it could be driven from both sides of the cab. Again the large front footstep and handrail are apparent.

(18) Sister engines 12052 and 12051, which were both built in BR days, at Derby. The early style of written ownership is displayed which therefore probably dates the view to the late 1940s. No 12052, nearest the camera, was first sent to Rugby before moving to Crewe and then Willesden, Nottingham, Toton, Westhouses and finally back to Crewe from where it ceased to work in June 1971. No 12051 was a month older but it too travelled widely, starting at Willesden and then to Nottingham, Toton, Westhouses, Newton Heath, Longsight, and finally Allerton. It too ceased work in 1971 but lasted a few months longer to October. It is not thought mileages were recorded for the shunters and instead servicing, etc, were based more on hours in service. The writing on the framing reads 'Hand Lamp Socket. Engine Sump oil Drain.' Notice no windscreen wipers are fitted.

(19) Another former LMS engine was No 12034, formerly No 7121, and proving the point about the type being able to be driven from either side of the cab. No location is given but from the wording on the first wagon, 'Runner Crewe', it is probably pretty safe to assume this was where it was photographed. Notice too in the background the unmistakable outline of a 'Duchess' pacific.

Above (20): This is the former LMS No 7074, as BR 12000, looking like it has been dumped at the end of a siding at some locomotive depot – note the coaling plant in the background. Electric marker lights for shunting and early BR 'cycling lion' crest plus electrification warning flashes. The whole adds up to perhaps a late 1950s or very early 1960s view, the last named embellishment coming in with the 25Kv overhead wires to Crewe around that time. This machine spent all its life at Crewe, firstly at North and then South and was withdrawn from the latter in April 1961. One final point of note is the compressed air whistle above the cab.

Opposite (21): At the same location but now almost certainly out of service – notice the planking at the cab door. Heavy balance weights to the wheels and whilst it may appear the sandboxes are missing their covers, this same item does not appear to be present in other images of the type. The large oval works plate bears the legend 'English Electric' at the top and 'Hawthorn Leslie' underneath with a date year in the centre. The man on the steam locomotive behind has literally been caught 'mid-step'.

(22) The same pairing as seen earlier, Nos 12051 and 12052, and seemingly a bit excessive in the motive power stakes for the small train. However, as this is clearly an engineer's working it is possible at one time the work involved might have necessitated an engine at either end. The single headlamp above the left hand buffer indicates a 'J' class working. Mutiple unit working was not provided.

(23) LMS No 7124 but renumbered as BR 12037 and yet to have the pre-nationalisation ownership decals removed. No date but likely at Crewe as this was its home depot until 1954. The chalk mark indicates 'Radiator Empty' so perhaps servicing/ maintenance is taking place. Minor damage to the front step handrail and, dare we say, typical grime livery. Shunters diesel or steam were certainly not a priority when it came to cleaning. In BR days after spells at Crewe and then Willesden, No 12034 spent 11 years at Chester from where it was withdrawn in October 1968.

(24) The end of the shunters – literally. An unidentified machine with LMR brake van and tail lamps for an unfitted freight. I think we can say with certainty the running rail on the left is not a transition curve! Notice on the underframe of the van the large box into which concrete or scrap iron would be housed in order to bring the weight up to the required amount and so allow the van to act as an effective brake.

Images 25 and 26: Apart from shunting engines and the well known 'twins', Nos 10001/10001, the LMS had also planned for the possible use of diesel traction on secondary and branch lines. Ordered as a single prototype from the North British Locomotive Company in 1946, No 10800 was completed and passed to British Railways in 1950. It utilised the Bo-Bo wheel arrangement with a cab towards one end and might even have been said to have design similarity with contemporary North American 'switcher' types although obviously conforming to the British loading gauge.

Power came from a 16 cylinder diesel engine producing 827hp at 1,250rpm. This was coupled to a DC generator which in turn drove four BTH axle-hung traction motors. As delivered livery was the BR standard for non shunter / non steam machines; black with silver for the running gear and roof. When clean this was also extremely smart but it was hardly practical in service and the silver was quickly replaced with more black.

Initially proving trials were carried out in Scotland but once formally accepted by the LMR it was allocated to Willesden. Here it regularly worked suburban traffic as far as Bletchley, a role which continued until transfer to the Southern Region in July 1952.

Power wise the engine was rated as comparable to a 'Class 3' steam engine with the intention that it would replace steam on secondary and branch line services. Visibility from the cab was poor for a diesel but again similar to that of a steam engine.

Reliability however was sometimes not good. Whether this was down to design, equipment, maintenance, or simple lack of familiarity is not totally clear, perhaps a combination of all. Certainly during its time on the Southern it was known as the 'wonder' locomotive. Not so much admiration of the technology but instead the rather cruel analogy 'I wonder if it will go today'.

No. 10800 it was returned from the Southern in December 1954 and was then tried out on Eastern Region services being based at Plaistow from where it worked transfer freight turns and also passenger services between Fenchurch Street and Southend although again reliability was poor.

Despite any misgivings BR were confident enough to order 54 similar locomotives that would become BR Classes 15 and 16 although these were delivered with an improved engine unit.

No 10800 survived until August 1959 when it was withdrawn but would shortly begin a new life as a prototype for Brush Traction and modified to use AC instead of DC power transmission. In its new guise it was given the name Hawk and with a new engine and transmission provided valuable experience which would later be incorporated into the Kestrel prototype. Hawk was used until 1968 but was stripped of its engine and main generator in 1972, the remains being finally scrapped in 1976.

(27) During its time on the Southern Region, No. 10800 is seen stripped down for repair/ overhaul at Brighton, 1 September 1953. When operating on the SR Brighton was usually the works to which the main line diesels, both ex LMR and the SR types were taken for attention when necessary.

(28 & 29): Having dealt with the 'little uns' (and the medium size 'un) we go back to the 'big uns' with an artist's impressions of how they were originally perceived to look both singly and as a pair. In reality the principal difference is at the nose end with that horrendous bulbous protrusion fortunately removed. Even so in both proposed and actual form there was some similarity with contemporary American styling. Note too the carriage type windows on the body side. Both artist's impressions are dated from early 1947 and marked 'Euston' so clearly these were produced with some idea as to what was to appear. Interestingly, contemporary information referring to the twin sets quotes '3,200hp and 100mph' although at the time their purpose was said to be for suburban and semi-fast passenger workings plus 'medium work' freight.

Opposite (30): We are back at a wet Euston again on 18 December 1947 for a further view of No 10000 with what appears to be a cover on the end of the single air horn. Oval buffers reduced the chance of buffer-lock when pushing on sharp curves although it will be noted there is only a vacuum and not an air brake hose connection. The engine hauled a demonstration train for representatives of the press to Watford and return.

Above (31): A different location, St Pancras this time, but fairly soon after. No 10000 again on its own and this time with an amount of bogie 'grime' apparent. The train is the 2.15pm departure – to Derby and Manchester Central and return, a duty it performed on a regular basis from 14 January 1948 to July 1948 during which time it had run 51,300 miles in six months, a credible mileage for a brand new design. The locomotive was still the subject of some interest wherever it appeared and also in the press, both technical and popular. Indeed one contemporary book / magazine aimed at the young enthusiast had the subject advising his mentor that he, "….wished to see one of those new fangled engines that were not powered by steam……"; the term 'diesel engine' not yet part of everyday language.

Left (32): No 10000 on a 'medium work' freight perhaps? More accurately a 'Class D Express freight'. Although certainly capable, the diesel was hampered in exactly the same way as steam on this type of working; not all the wagons of the train being braked. Not necessarily in this instance, but it was all too easy for the diesel driver to unintentionally exceed the preferred speed for this type of train which might result in a hot axle box on a following wagon. There are several reasons why No 10000 might be on this turn; a test or trial, part of the regular diagram in the Autumn / Winter months (see later comment), a means to move the engine from 'A' to 'B' and earn revenue at the same time, or the engine was suffering a defect rendering it (temporarily) unsuitable for passenger working.

Left (33) Control desk of No 10000. The main controller had eight notches with the recommendation that positions 3, 6 and 8 were the optimum for obtaining the most power from the engine – the engine would run at 620rpm in notches 3 to 6 inclusive. (The firing order of the 'V' shaped 16 cylinder engine was 1F, 8B, 5F, 4B, 7F, 2B, 3F, 6B, 8F, 1B, 4F, 5B, 2F, 7B, 6F, 3B.) One criticism of the engine was that the vacuum exhauster was not considered particularly efficient by some drivers; a rapid brake application meaning the exhauster would not operate quickly enough to blow off the brakes resulting in stopping short of the intended point. For this reason drivers would learn to make several short brake applications when slowing.

Opposite (34 and inset 35): Refuelling was obviously different to, and a lot easier, than for steam. Again an early image and for no other reason that the bogies are yet to receive their coating of workaday grime. No location is given so mention should be made that refuelling was sometimes by the simple method of connecting a pipe from a nearby rail wagon. As necessary, water would also have to be taken for the train heat boiler.

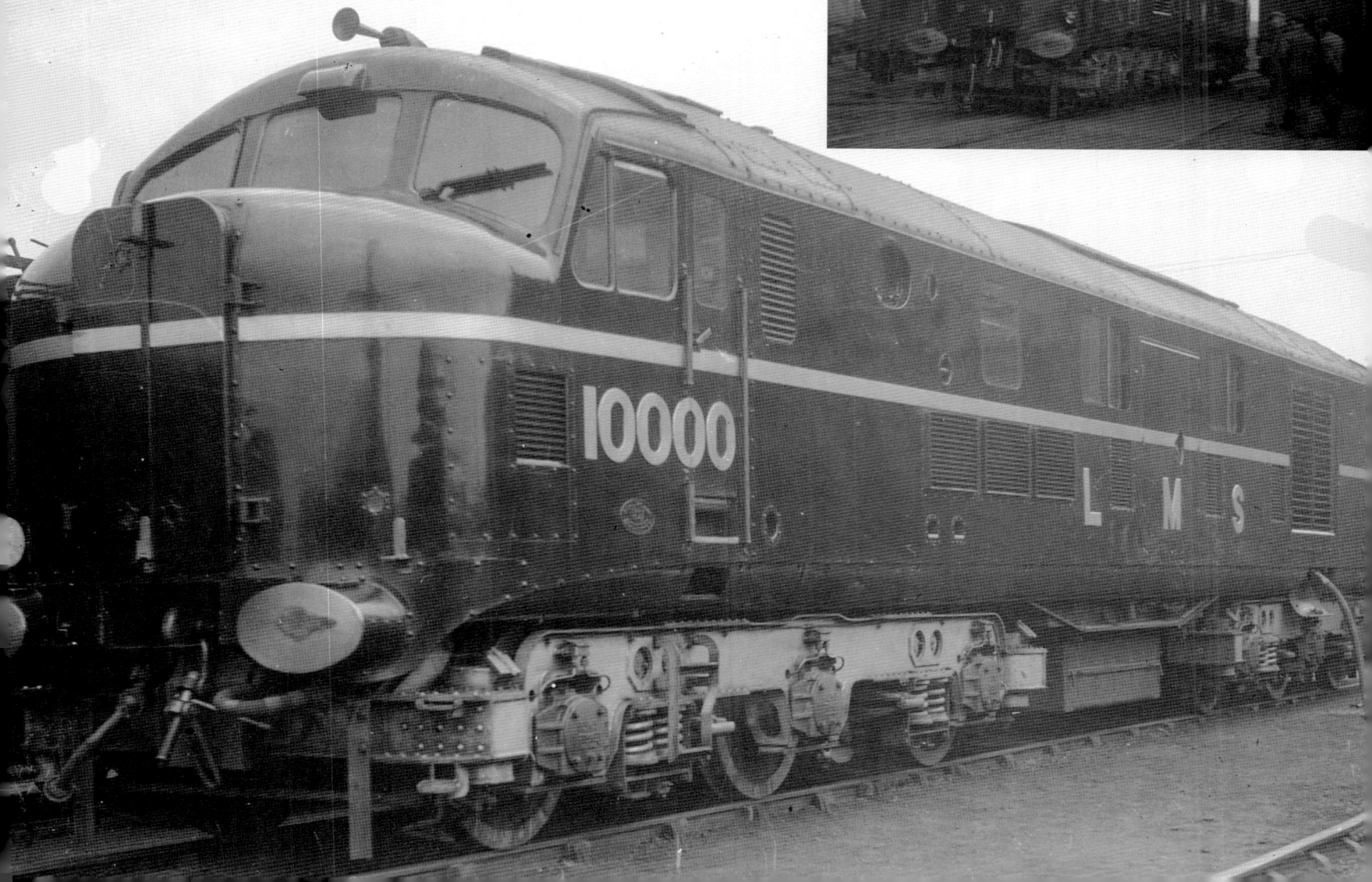

(36) No 10000 in what is clearly a steam roundhouse – Camden perhaps? At this time, everyday maintenance of the diesel fleet was carried out in either a steam environment or else in the open air, neither particularly ideal. The Western Region would learn the same lesson, especially with gas turbine No 18000. It would take investment in modern airy and clean conditions to really improve matters but that in turn would not come until there was a sufficient fleet of diesels operating to justify the expense.

(37) A final view (for now) of No 10000, running solo and with company letters displayed. These were naturally removed soon into the British Railways regime.

Left (38): The second engine to identical design, appropriately No 10001, was completed in early 1948 and consequently emerged with no evidence of ownership. The engine is seen here on Camden bank. In his 1957 book *Top Link Locomotives* by Norman McKillop, Norman describes a run on the LMS diesel leaving Euston with the comment that compared with a steam locomotive the diesel would top Camden bank at 40mph against 20-25mph for steam and have reached 50mph just over two miles from the start.

Above (39): The pair together on the Up 'Royal Scot' at Carpenters Park on 2 June 1949 – the design was never multiplied further although the same power unit was developed and uprated further to be used in the Southern Region pairing of 10201 and 10202 at 1,750hp and then finally in a third SR machine, No 10203, at 2,000hp. Notice the connecting doors are open – presumably clipped back as well to prevent rattling. This would allow the 'fireman' to attend to any necessary adjustments on the second engine with both controlled by the one driver on the lead engine. Instructions issued as to maintenance stated that in freezing conditions and if stabled, ideally this should be under cover and positioned so the radiator was not head on to the wind. Other comments mentioned that should there be the need to drain the radiator then this must not take place until the engine had been shut down for two hours.

Above (40): Carpenters Road in pouring rain – the engines also had wipers. The front 'nose' or 'bonnet', to use the American term, was intended to reduce the flashing effect to the driver's eyes of the sleepers, in reality it contained just two components, a compressor and a traction motor blower – plus of course the space for the corridor connection. Whilst the latter was considered a necessary inclusion in the first diesel designs, in reality it was a nuisance to the crew, being a regular source of draughts.

Opposite (41): Bushey, again on 2 June 1949 and the same train as previous, the Up 'Royal Scot'. The load on this service could well be 16 coaches, the same trailing weight as was given to a 'Duchess' working the service – no concessions being made for the diesels.

(42) Another long train for the pairing. Despite not bearing the original company lettering, the livery of both was otherwise identical. With two locomotives now available it was understandable the London Midland Region would want to try them together on heavier turns and both were sent to Camden in October 1948, working between Euston and Carlisle from 4 October. Unfortunately it was not an totally auspicious start as just five days later No 10000 failed and had to be returned to Derby.

(43): In the 'Fell country'. It must be said the LMS engines were very much a test bed for the future and it would certainly not be fair to say their performance or reliability were faultless. One problem that emerged very early on was oil leakage from the cylinder head and crankcase cover and which certainly did not help towards maintenance when the engine room could be a place covered in oil. Not for no reason were the early diesels renowned for depositing oil all over the system – but then again the Southern engines were little, if any, better.

Top (44): Another issue was that of the train heat boiler. Naturally these were oil fired but turned out to be somewhat unreliable in railway service although absolutely fine elsewhere. The issue was purely that of the railway environment, horizontal and vertical stresses meaning the relays and pumps quickly became unreliable when running at speed – not exactly the ideal way of promoting the new form of traction to the travelling public. The pairing are seen here on a dull 12 August 1959, No 10000 still with LMS insignia, at Carlisle and about to take over a Blackpool to Glasgow service.

Bottom (45): The same train with the pairing now attached (the train had been brought in by Black 5, No 45484). Despite the earlier comments the steam from the boiler seems to indicate all might be well in that department – for the present at least, but there again the engines are stationary. It was this heating issue that meant the pair were put on to freight working, likely individually, in the winter months. When rostered as a pair for a passenger turn, should one not be available. The remaining working engine was then usually transferred away from the LNWR back to the Midland main line to continue working until its twin was once again back in service.

Opposite (46): At speed with the 'Royal Scot'. This was a regular turn when both engines were available for traffic with both also allocated to Willesden.

(47): Still attracting attention! One of the problems with the diesels was that the turns they worked meant men in the top link were required to learn the new traction but with only two available also only drove them on an irregular basis. Consequently it was not always a happy time and some failures in service were in fact simply down to lack of familiarity - and forgetfulness. It should have been better as the working conditions were (should have been) a lot more comfortable. One slightly sad example was the Derby driver who continuing to lean out of the cabside window of the diesel on the whole journey to St Pancras – exactly as he did when driving a steam engine.

(48) With the two engines coupled together overall length was somewhat longer than a 'Duchess', whilst individually each machine weighed 130.6 tons which, carried over six axles, meant an axle weight of 22.2 tons. This was still less than the steam engine but somewhat higher than an individual steam engine of comparable power. The LMS and LMR placed a single diesel in the 5MT criteria although, when taking into account the acceleration and hill climbing ability, in practice the results were more akin to a steam engine in at least 'Class 6' criteria.

Opposite top (49) Early BR days. The silver roofs show up well here, something else that developed a grey exhaust and oil stained tinge as time passed. Mention has previously been made of the credible mileage run by No 10000 alone in the first few months of 1948, whilst in service the main issues appear to have been with the fuel injection equipment, timing chains and turbo chargers. When working in multiple, banking was rarely provided from Euston or on the Shap, Tebay and Beattock banks, even with loads in excess of 500 tons, although if a single engine were employed on such a duty then assistance might well be provided on Shap and Beattock. (Note 'banking' and not a pilot – the reason being that a steam engine pilot ahead might well result in ash and cinders being sucked into the air intakes of the diesel behind.)

Opposite bottom (50): Not quite the same rake of coaches – were many trains ever made up of the same stock on a regular basis? We have no figures available for fuel consumption whilst working as a pair but individually on freight duties and based over 39,65 hours, fuel usage was 123,943 gallons for 136,439 miles; equivalent to slightly less than 1 gallon per mile. The fuel used was ordinary diesel and not the heavy 'Bunker C' type product used in the WR Gas Turbine No 18000 nor in the oil burning steam engines of 1946-51.

Above (51): Paired again and interesting to note how the handrail is cut to allow prefedence to the engine number. Folklore has it that when the pair were first coupled together and an attempt made to move both from a single cab, the engineers were not totally certain they would move in the same direction - luckily they did! Whilst this may sound much akin to a circus it must be recalled that this period in history was very much pushing technology to the limit so far as the application of diesel power to a main line railway environment was concerned. Notice here the connecting doors between the engines are open but according to David Clough in his work *Pioneer Diesels* (Ian Allan 2005) this was not always the case for the reasons of draughts previously mentioned. This might seem a slightly strange comment to make as the crew would have been at the front of the lead engine and so not thought likely to have been affected. To be fair the draught was also probably not much worse than that for a passenger moving between contemporary coaching stock. The connecting doors would of course have to be set in the open position before the train was in motion.

Opposite (52), this page (53): In disgrace at Harrow. No 10000 reported as failed whilst in charge of the 1.35p. Euston to Perth. Regretfully we have no date, no details of the failure, and no information as to whether this was a single or multiple unit turn. What is more certain is this could have been the only time one of the latest examples of modern motive power was seen in a coal siding!

This page (54), opposite (55): Under repair at Brighton having run in the order of 400,000 miles. From the same chalk mark on the right hand buffer both views also taken at the same time and with the engine unit removed. In the foreground is the unmistakable outline of a Bulleid front bogie. As mentioned, when operating on the Southern, repairs were mostly undertaken at Brighton but on the LMS it was the responsibility of Derby.

Top (56) and bottom (57): The twins being shunted at Derby, no date but the later BR crest will be noted on the sides. Tail lamp attached lower centre on No. 10000.

Opposite (58): In charge of 'The Royal Scot' at Preston on 13 November 1958 and showing the twins were still considered as suitable for front line services a decade after their introduction. This was despite the introduction in the same year of the first of the BR Type 4 D200 series diesels. Although excellent engines in their own right, the D200 series only produced 2,000hp whilst the LMS pairing was 3,300hp. Indeed when first introduced the abilities of the D200 series were decidedly inferior to that of a steam 'Princess' or 'Duchess'. Of course the latter was dependent upon the condition of the engine, the quality of the coal and the ability of the crew. The diesel engines seen might be deemed modern but the same could hardly be said for that station footbridge!

This page (59) opposite (60): In charge of 'The Royal Scot' at Preston, both views taken on 4 June 1959 and where some modernisation in the form of the new canopy has been provided.

Opposite (61): Whether this has anything to do with the images of the failed No 10000 seen previously is not known. Certainly London area - as per the fourth rail system - and definitely temporary assistance as the steam engine - a BR Class 4MT 2-6-4T is coupled ahead of the diesel.

Above (62): Passing Wolverhampton No 3 signal box. Notice the position of the BR emblem; according to period placed above or below the centre line. On what appears to be a dry day, the second man may well have little physical work to undertake on the engine. Almost everything visible in the photograph has not disappeared; the engine, the rolling stock and the signal box, all consigned to history.

It was a great pity that none of the pioneer diesels, LMS and SR survived for posterity. One at least should as a link to the development of modern traction. Unfortunately in the 1960s railway motive power heritage was definitely tuned into preserving steam and the opportunity to save one of the LMS 'twins' even by officialdom was let slip. In more modern time a group has been formed to promote the construction of a 'new build' 10000.

Top (63): Suburban duty perhaps for No. 10001, certainly this would appear to be confirmed from the single lamp 'below the chimney'. Individually each locomotive was equal to a Class 5 steam engine, a 'Jubilee' or 'Black 5' but twas far better than steam on uphill gradients.

Bottom (64): Birmingham New Street with the following carriages complete with roof boards - unfortunately unable to be read. Both locomotives were out of service for almost the whole of 1956 pending availability of spares. This had been exasperated as English Electric had now ceased production of the power unit fitted. Obviously the problem was overcome as the engines continued to work beyond that date but this inability to locate spares did little to endear the dieselisation programme that was just commencing.

Freight turns.

Top (65): The engines were often to be found on freight during winter due to their train heating boilers either failing or not being found satisfactory. Here No. 10000 is passing Hatch End fairly early in its career, 28 December 1951, with a fully fitted working.

Bottom (66): A similar working with the same engine in charge. Notice the two ro-ro milk tanks in the consist. General availability of the pair was good, equal to 66% for No.10000 and 65% for No. 10001. This equated to just in excess of 128,000 miles each in 1958 - also their best year. Taken as an average over their life span, the figure for No. 10000 overt 15 years was 57,000 miles per annum and for No. 10001 with its longer 18 year life, 56,000 miles. In the London area anything other than routine maintenance was carried out at Stonebridge Park as it was recognised the pair had more in common with an electric set rather than a steam engine.

(67): Sometime around 1957, the pair received BR green livery relived by an orange/black/orange stripe at the lower and mid body lines. As with any railway livery, it was very smart when freshly applied but cleaning standards were certainly not to general pre-war standards during this period with BR struggling to recruit footplate staff. Perhaps the strangest addition to the livery was a primrose yellow painted roof. This does not show up in black and white but colour views of the period confirm the colour. Why such a shade should have been selected when oily exhaust fumes would be present the moment the engines were started cannot be imagined.

(68): Showing off its primrose roof to advantage, No. 10001 also has a travelling fitter on board. Possibly then a test run after repair.

Left (69): In final form / livery complete with small yellow warning panel, perhaps it was fortunate neither ever went into BR blue. Externally we cannot be certain if there were minor differences between the two engines or indeed if external changes were made over the years. One that might have occurred concerns the shield surrounding the coupling hook which does appear different here compared with other images.

Top (70): End of the line for No. 10000 at Derby. It had been withdrawn week ended 7 December 1963. Whether this was due to a specific defect or, as mentioned below, intentionally to provide a source of spares for the sister engine is not certain. It languished here for a further four years before being sold for scrap to J Cashmore of Newport and had met its end by April 1968.

Bottom (71): No. 10001 separated from its sister but seen here also withdrawn at Willesden. This engine had been kept in service until week ending 12 March 1966 having previously been observed in Derby diesel repair shop two months earlier. Perhaps the requisite spares donated from No. 10000 had by now simply run out. It remained stored until January 1968 when it was sold to Cox & Danks of Acton and cut up at their location in February 1968 having run about 1,000,000 in service. Note the livery on both has relapsed with a singe band around the centre.

FELL DIESEL MECHANICAL LOCOMOTIVE

LAYOUT OF PROTOTYPE LOCOMOTIVE
(BRITISH RAILWAYS No. 10,100)

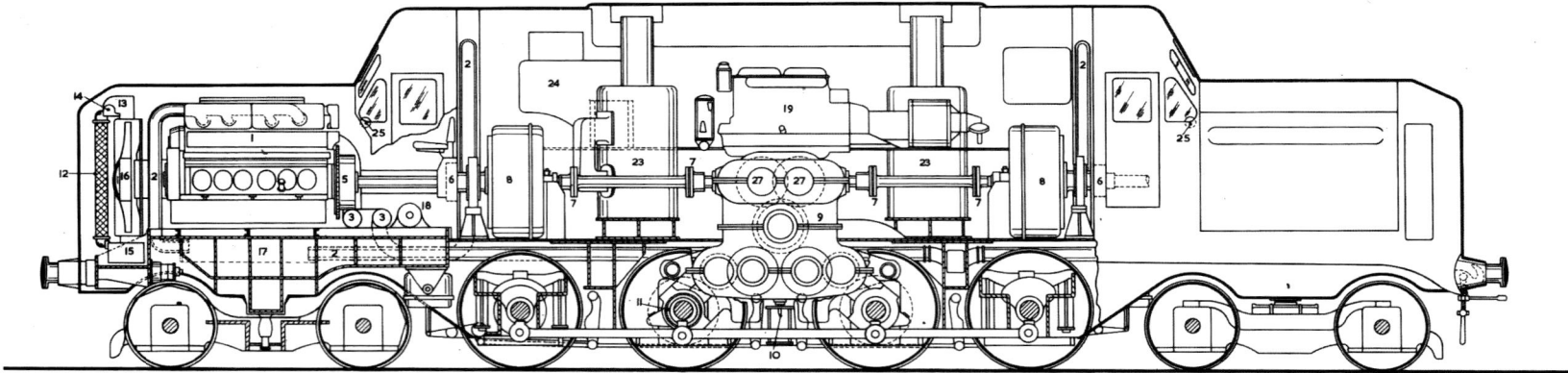

1	500 H.P. DAVEY PAXMAN 12 R.P.H. DIESEL ENGINES.	8	FLUID COUPLINGS, TYPE S.C.R.5. SIZE Nº 36	15	BOTTOM TANKS.	22	VACUUM EXHAUSTERS.

No.	Description	No.	Description	No.	Description	No.	Description
1	500 H.P. DAVEY PAXMAN 12 R.P.H. DIESEL ENGINES.	8	FLUID COUPLINGS, TYPE S.C.R.5. SIZE Nº 36	15	BOTTOM TANKS.	22	VACUUM EXHAUSTERS.
2	EXHAUST PIPES FOR 12 R.P.H. DIESEL ENGINES.	9	GEARBOX.	16	RADIATOR FAN.	23	TRAIN HEATING BOILERS.
3	SUPERCHARGE AIR PIPES FOR 12 R.P.H. DIESEL ENGINES.	10	REVERSING CONNECTION.	17	DIESEL OIL FUEL TANKS (CAPACITY 720 GALLONS.)	24	TRAIN HEATING BOILERS WATER TANKS. (CAP.ʸ 500 GALLS.)
4	WATER CIRCULATING PUMPS.	11	QUILL DRIVING SHAFT.	18	LIFTING BRACKETS.	25	LOCOMOTIVE CONTROLS.
5	BIBBY COUPLINGS.	12	RADIATORS. (WATER ELEMENTS. OIL ELEMENTS.)	19	150 H.P. A.E.C. DIESEL AUXILIARY ENGINES.	26	CLUTCH TO RELEASE ABUTMENT OF ONE S.S.S. COUPLING.
6	LAYRUB COUPLINGS.	13	WATER HEADER TANKS.	20	BEVEL GEAR BOXES FOR AUXILIARY SHAFT DRIVE.	27	SYNCHRO SELF SHIFTING COUPLINGS
7	LAYRUB COUPLINGS.	14	OIL TOP MANIFOLD.	21	HOLMES CONNERSVILLE SUPERCHARGE BLOWERS.		

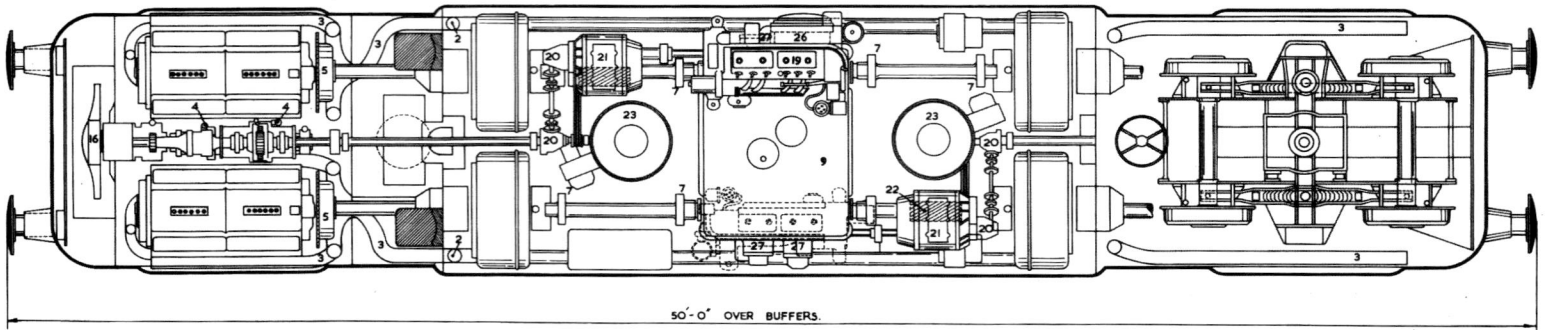

50'-0" OVER BUFFERS.

Opposite (72): Plan, above (73): Official view of the 'Fell' as built with 4-8-4 (2-D-2) wheel arrangement. Traction was from four separate engine units produced by Davey Paxman. As conceived these were to have been of 400hp each but as fitted they were rated at 500hp each so giving a total of 2,000hp and resulting in the most powerful diesel locomotive to run on a British railway up to that time. The individual engines were intended to be switched in or out of use according to demand, one each being mounted at each end with two in the centre. All four engines were linked and whilst it could never be 100% certain that all four would actually operate at the exact same speed, the presence of differential couplings ensured any disparity did not affect performance. The use of four separate engines allied to the inter-connecting couplings did mean the disadvantage of added complexity but on the plus side it meant that should an engine fail, the train could still continue to destination although at reduced speed. Confidence in diesel was still perhaps slightly uncertain.

(74): In partial undress with the complexities associated with the four separate engines visible. Below the framing the final drive was by a train of gears. Reversing was by vacuum operated sliding dog clutches. As such the engine could run equally well in either direction.

(75): The heart of the engine, the gearbox designed by Fell and mounted on to the centre pair of driving axles / wheels after final checking of the cranks and gearwheels. The massive balance weights necessary to compensate for the connecting rods will be noted.

Top: (76): Contemporary view of the engine at Marylebone during inspection / trials. The Fell engine, named after its innovator, Lt. Col. L F R Fell C.Eng., F.I.Mech.E. (ex Doncaster apprentice), was an attempt to maintain the flexibility of the steam engine so far as power characteristics were concerned whilst using a diesel engine for the power source. E V Richards in his book for the RCTS *LMS Diesel Locomotives and Railcars*, comments as to whether the engine would have been built at all under true LMS jurisdiction but by signing an agreement in October 1947 the die was in effect cast. Even so it was still up to the Ministry of Transport to give permission for BR to proceed with a single prototype. The engine is seen here at Marylebone for inspection on 23 May 1951 having been towed from Derby by a new Standard Class 4 No. 75000. Unlike No. 10000 however, there was no publicity 'first run'. The technicians with their spotless overalls would not always be that clean - perhaps they used a particular brand of washing powder!

Bottom: (77): As with the intended trials of No. 10000 against a 'Duchess', so No. 10100 as it was identified, was to be trialled against No. 10000. Again this did not take place although test working was undertaken with varying loads. Prior to the London inspection, No. 10100 was noted at Derby as 'almost complete' in August 1950 although the trail now goes cold until it worked its first trains the short distance between Derby and Lock Lane Sidings, via Chellaston Junction on 9 January 1951. It would be tempting to speculate as to the five month delay, especially as prior to this it had appeared almost complete some months earlier. Trial running continued at intervals during 1951 interspersed with works visits and long periods out of use. The engine was formerly added to LMR stock week ending 19 January 1952 thereafter running both test and service trains. It is seen here on an unreported date at Manchester Central.

Opposite (78): Derby, 21 April 1955. Livery was all over black with the cab handrails painted white. Minor livery changes occurred throughout its life including going into green circa March 1957 whilst the BR logo changed around the latter time and the position of the cab numbers also varied. As with all the diesels mentioned in this book, none ever carried names. Compared with Nos. 10000/10001, the Fell was short; 50 feet against 61 feet. Even so oval buffers were fitted.

(79): In service much time was spent on the former Midland main line, as here where the engine is seen at Didsbury with a morning Manchester to Derby express. Folklore has it the first time the engine worked over this route to Manchester it arrived at destination covered in soot; consequent upon a century's accumulation being blasted off the various tunnel roofs by the diesel exhausts allied to the none too streamlined front end design. (Mr Bulleid experienced the same on the Southern in 1940 when he fitted two and then three chimneys to a steam engine in an attempt to disperse exhaust steam more efficiently. It was not sucessful and was not replicated.)

(80): Conveniently identified as Chapel-en-le-Frith Central, No. 10100 is seen with a single local head code. An early view as all the axles are coupled. Unconfirmed, but are the housings on the front electric headlights? Visibility with the long bonnet ahead cannot have been good during coupling operations. In practical terms the engine worked between Manchester Central and Derby, between Manchester Central and Liverpool - the route taken requiring various unspecified structures to be altered to allow its passage, test trains over the Settle & Carlisle and to Willesden and Eastbourne (see images 83 and 84), the last named for exhibition purposes.

(81) Passing Tebay with a test train for Crewe after having traversed the Settle & Carlisle line. This was one a series of trails which had commenced on 25 April 1955 and involved a Dynamometer car (seen here as the first vehicle) as well as the LMR Mobile Test Unit. On one of these tests the 18 miles from Appleby to Ais Gill were covered in just over 25 minutes with 389 tons in tow. Using full throttle 1,900hp was measured at the drawbar at 44mph, a commendable achievement considering a theoretical 100hp was all that was left to move the locomotive itself as well as cover traction losses. The starting tractive effort was recorded at 29,400lbs or just over 13 tons. Fuel consumption was said to be equal to the first pair of SR diesels, Nos. 10101/2, but no actual figures are given. (The nominal 2,000hp rating quoted should be read with caution as formal documentation of the time refers to '…total installed power for traction 2,060hp…' and '…total power for supercharging and auxiliary drives 300hp.') Note the mention that the engines were mechanically supercharged rather than being turbocharged.

(82) The low angle shot accentuates the engine bulk, visually perhaps not helped by its restricted length. The original design has planned for two train heat boilers to be fitted but the LMR has insisted the engine be kept to 50 feet and as such there was only room for one. Even so it was fitted with a bi-directional water scoop so as to be able to replenish the water tank whilst running. No images have emerged of the engine working other than passenger trains. The service is the 12.05pm Derby to St Pancras on 20 March 1952 and is seen at Loughborough Midland.

Top (83), bottom (84): On Saturday, 2 June 1951 British Railways played host to the International Union of Railways (UIC) exhibition whose conference was being held at Eastbourne. A number of examples of the latest motive power and rolling stock running on BR were on display at the station which included No. 10100.

Visits to the display was restricted to the delegates for the morning, although the public were allowed access in the afternoon. (The UIC had been formed in 1922 with the aim of standardising industry practice certainly amongst adjoining countries whose rail networks might conjoin.)

The designer of No. 10100 Lt. Col Fell was present together with his two sisters and as reported in the contemporary press '… assisted his 89-year-old mother on to the footplate' (no doubt of his own design).

No. 10100 had been towed to Eastbourne by brand new Standard Class 5 No. 73001, arriving (presumable via Willesden) and thence through Brent, Barnes and Battersea Yard. It was similarly towed back after the event although this time by another new engine, No. 75000.

(85) No. 10100 was on display again, this time for the International Railway Congress at Willesden from 25 May to 4 June 1954. Basic technical details are given on the information board which states a maximum speed of 75mph and a weight of 120 tons. Alongside is Western Region gas turbine No. 18000. Being a one-off, No. 10100 was not fitted for multiple working. Livery was gloss black and possibly especially for the exhibition, the outside cranks were painted bright red.

(86): This time the engine appears dwarfed by the bulk of Manchester Central station where is was photographed in January 1955. Already more than half way through its life, if it were known No. 10100 had less than three years of working left as on 16 October 1958 the train heat boiler caught fire at this station whilst the engine was waiting to work the 12.25pm train to Derby. Although a fire extinguisher system was fitted this could not cope with the inferno and the local fire brigade were called for. Needless to say No. 10100 was unable to continue and instead the engine made its way to Derby for assessment. Although no longer involved in the day to day operations and trails of his engine, Col Fell must have regarded the failure with some sadness. Ironic too that what would turn out to be the death of his engine was not caused by anything associated with his actual design. Not surprisingly Fell had made plans for a Mk 2 version although details are scant. With contemporary thoughts also turning to high speed diesels he had also proposed a 4-6-0+4-6-0 machine which would have developed 3,800hp and been able to run at 120mph. BR's comparative power requirement for the same speed was indicated to be 4,000hp. Unfortunately neither did the design, original or proposed, result in any orders from overseas railways.

(87): Presumably as with all the early diesels it was practice for a travelling fitter to be on board, certainly this was until reliability had been established - or perhaps cruelly until the novelty wore off and it was decided the cost was not justified. Whatever, these men were often seen in white or light coloured overalls hence the man on the platform may well be undertaking this task. At some point it appears the centre cab window may have been deliberately blackened.

Left (88): On the road again, although we cannot tell whether this is a test or service train. Despite its novelty, No. 10100 was popular with its drivers due to its hill climbing ability but perhaps also because their role whilst driving was certainly far easier compared with a steam engine. Other plus features included the smooth starting characteristics. The lack of body length though meant it was a decidedly cramped machine to work on.

Above (89): Confidentially working a named train; there does not appear to have been any space or indeed time when a headboard was carried, No. 10100 passes 8F No. 48696. The Fell had originally been given the same power classification as the LMS twins, namely 5P5F but this was later increased for No. 10100 to 6P5F.

(90): Leaning to the curve with a St Pancras - Derby working. Contemporary technical details, (Col Fell along with the engine builders were clearly keen to publicise their achievement) mention the considered positive aspect of being able to cut in or out engines. There were though restrictions to the speed range possible with limited engines engaged. On one engine; 0-6mph. Two engines 6-17mph. Three engines 17-24mph. Four engines 24-78mph. (No doubt the '75mph' quoted on the display board at Willesden was for convenience. In similar fashion the weight quoted in the manual was 116 tons.)

Top (91), bottom (92): Under repair at Derby. Perhaps not surprisingly for a single prototype, much time was spent in works. One unfortunate defect occurred when owing to a misunderstanding the engine went out with no oil in the axle boxes. Even so it managed some 900 miles in this state until a seizure occurred resulting in bend rods.

According to John Cove formerly a director of Davey Paxman & Co, the locomotive was extensively tested and did prove the viability of an entirely mechanical drive for a locomotive of this power. "However, in retrospect it is my opinion that a mistake was made in deciding that everything on board should be mechanically driven as this led to a complex and troublesome arrangement of long shafts driving auxiliaries such as the radiator fans. The positioning of the radiators at the ends of the locomotive also caused problems. Air supply to and from the trailing radiator which was partially blanked off by an attached carriage was marginal at best, and cross connections to compensate for this, coupled with the need to include cooling for four main and two auxiliary engines resulted in a very complex system that gave a lot of problems with air venting and overheating. There was the problem of the AEC auxiliary engines and the Rootes blowers they drove to supercharge the main engines. In a station, with maximum boost required for starting the train from rest the noise from these was hideous, especially as it was added to the noise caused by the radiator fans and six engines also running. At that time a number of competitors were running various other prototypes on British Rail and when the Fell locomotive passed them their service engineers always made a point of ostentatiously blocking their ears!"

According to Col Fell, at some stage the gearbox suffered failure which had resulted from relatively small beginnings. It started with the failure of a bolt in its upper part. Fell recounts, "I cannot recall whether this was attributable to faulty design, materials or workmanship but the main point was that the broken bits passed all the way down through the gear train and rendered most of the gear wheels unfit for further service."

Writing some years later, Col Fell, an understandably disappointed perhaps even embittered man added, (When failures occurred) "The authorities in London had no interest in the further development of the Fell system as the policy at the time was to build steam locomotives exclusively. No. 10100 no longer enjoyed any priority in the shops. The gearbox took as long to repair as it took to built the complete locomotive." (The latter comment probably attributable to the two years the engine spent out of service from August 1955 until August 1957.)

Left (93): Derby Works in the Spring of 1954. Whether the Fell was regarded a success or otherwise remains open to debate. The time to have multiplied the design would have been the early 1950s but then there was neither the money nor the will which also goes to explain why further examples of the LMS and SR designs (and similarly the WR gas turbine) were not produced at this time. It would take the 1955 Modernisation Plan before any real progress was made and the Fell was by then likely seen as too complicated compared with any advantages it may have offered again a diesel with electric drive.

Above (94): Following the Manchester fire the engine was dumped in the shed yard at Derby. It had been purchased by BR in 1955 and so was theirs to do with as they wished. With the choice made not to multiply the design, the decision had probably already been taken to keep the engine in service until a major defect occurred or similar major repair was necessary. Clearly the fire was that catalyst although without knowing the amount of resultant damage we might question why the engine could not then have been restricted to freight turns? Perhaps the fire had damaged far more than simply the train heat boiler. It was officially withdrawn week ending 22 November 1958 and after being slowly dismantled was finally scrapped in July 1960 It had run some 100,000 miles in just over five actual years in traffic.

(95): Certainly not an LMS design, but the Southern Railway had ordered a pair of main line diesels ahead of the LMS going in for theirs. On the SR there was only a small, albeit excellent design team for the project led by Percy Bollen at Ashford, hence with fewer staff the design took longer to complete. "George Ivatt will tell me how he gets on," thought Bulleid and he did. (H. 'George' Ivatt was CME of the LMS and also Bulleid's brother-in-law.) With the LMS No 10000 coming out about 10 tons overweight on two six-wheeled bogies and with a large proportion of deadweight (ie not spring-borne), Bulleid was glad he had time to get his right. Might it even have been the design to get Bulleid interested in diesel traction for the first time? (Evidently not - witness the Turf Burner in Ireland later!) When LMS No. 10000 was reported to have damaged the road entering St Pancras, that was it and radical thoughts were needed on avoiding a similar situation. Baker, Percy's number two, remembered Bulleid and Bollen being cloistered all day but emerging with exactly what was needed, a neat carrying axle on to which there would be no problem getting the increased weight, all thanks to the centreless bogie being used. On the diesel there was nowhere to centre a conventional Bissell truck so Bulleid, who was familiar with Gresley's swing-link arrangement for hoisting the 'V2's into a curve, turned this on its side with the link pins on the buffer beam; result as neat a solution as could be. "Up and down movements…..?" Percy might have queried, and then answered himself "Silentblocs!" (mountings) "Of course," OVB agreed. There was another advantage in not being the first; the EE Co had got the engine output up to 1,750 hp, a useful power increment. There would be three SR diesels, Nos 10201 and 10202 with 1,750hp engines, and a third No. 10203 rated at 2,000hp. All three were transferred to the LMR in 1954/55 and lasted out their days working alongside the LMS design - but never in multiple. All three similarly met their end in the 1960s. No. 10201 is seen here at Willesden on a Euston to Bletchley service on 16 July 1960.